Royal Circus epitomized.

Charles Dibdin

Royal Circus epitomized.
Dibdin, Charles
ESTCID: T045260
Reproduction from British Library
The author's prefatory letter signed: C. Dibdin. An account of the quarrel between the manager, Dibdin and the lessee of the Royal Circus, William Davis.
London : printed for the author and sold by all booksellers in Lo[ndon and] Westminster, 1784.
xx,79,[1]p. ; 4°

Gale ECCO Print Editions

Relive history with *Eighteenth Century Collections Online*, now available in print for the independent historian and collector. This series includes the most significant English-language and foreign-language works printed in Great Britain during the eighteenth century, and is organized in seven different subject areas including literature and language; medicine, science, and technology; and religion and philosophy. The collection also includes thousands of important works from the Americas.

The eighteenth century has been called "The Age of Enlightenment." It was a period of rapid advance in print culture and publishing, in world exploration, and in the rapid growth of science and technology – all of which had a profound impact on the political and cultural landscape. At the end of the century the American Revolution, French Revolution and Industrial Revolution, perhaps three of the most significant events in modern history, set in motion developments that eventually dominated world political, economic, and social life.

In a groundbreaking effort, Gale initiated a revolution of its own: digitization of epic proportions to preserve these invaluable works in the largest online archive of its kind. Contributions from major world libraries constitute over 175,000 original printed works. Scanned images of the actual pages, rather than transcriptions, recreate the works ***as they first appeared.***

Now for the first time, these high-quality digital scans of original works are available via print-on-demand, making them readily accessible to libraries, students, independent scholars, and readers of all ages.

For our initial release we have created seven robust collections to form one the world's most comprehensive catalogs of 18th century works.

Initial Gale ECCO Print Editions collections include:

History and Geography
Rich in titles on English life and social history, this collection spans the world as it was known to eighteenth-century historians and explorers. Titles include a wealth of travel accounts and diaries, histories of nations from throughout the world, and maps and charts of a world that was still being discovered. Students of the War of American Independence will find fascinating accounts from the British side of conflict.

Social Science
Delve into what it was like to live during the eighteenth century by reading the first-hand accounts of everyday people, including city dwellers and farmers, businessmen and bankers, artisans and merchants, artists and their patrons, politicians and their constituents. Original texts make the American, French, and Industrial revolutions vividly contemporary.

Medicine, Science and Technology
Medical theory and practice of the 1700s developed rapidly, as is evidenced by the extensive collection, which includes descriptions of diseases, their conditions, and treatments. Books on science and technology, agriculture, military technology, natural philosophy, even cookbooks, are all contained here.

Literature and Language
Western literary study flows out of eighteenth-century works by Alexander Pope, Daniel Defoe, Henry Fielding, Frances Burney, Denis Diderot, Johann Gottfried Herder, Johann Wolfgang von Goethe, and others. Experience the birth of the modern novel, or compare the development of language using dictionaries and grammar discourses.

Religion and Philosophy
The Age of Enlightenment profoundly enriched religious and philosophical understanding and continues to influence present-day thinking. Works collected here include masterpieces by David Hume, Immanuel Kant, and Jean-Jacques Rousseau, as well as religious sermons and moral debates on the issues of the day, such as the slave trade. The Age of Reason saw conflict between Protestantism and Catholicism transformed into one between faith and logic -- a debate that continues in the twenty-first century.

Law and Reference
This collection reveals the history of English common law and Empire law in a vastly changing world of British expansion. Dominating the legal field is the *Commentaries of the Law of England* by Sir William Blackstone, which first appeared in 1765. Reference works such as almanacs and catalogues continue to educate us by revealing the day-to-day workings of society.

Fine Arts
The eighteenth-century fascination with Greek and Roman antiquity followed the systematic excavation of the ruins at Pompeii and Herculaneum in southern Italy; and after 1750 a neoclassical style dominated all artistic fields. The titles here trace developments in mostly English-language works on painting, sculpture, architecture, music, theater, and other disciplines. Instructional works on musical instruments, catalogs of art objects, comic operas, and more are also included.

ROYAL CIRCUS

EPITOMIZED.

LONDON:

Printed for the AUTHOR

And ſold by all Bookſellers in Lo

Weſtminſter. 1784

PRICE TWO SHILLINGS AND SIXPENCE.

TO

William Davis, Efq;

SIR,

AS you prevailed upon your friends to build the Circus, folely with a view to ferve me; as you have repeatedly promifed that place fhould make me independent for life; and declared how happy you were to find an opportunity of effentially affifting an old friend, whofe abilities you had an opinion of, and from whofe acquaintance you received

a plea-a pleaſure, I cannot ſo properly dedicate the following narrative to any perſon as yourſelf.

INDEED it addreſſes itſelf to you in every page. You ſigned a memorandum, inſuring me my ſituation; you exacted my implicit reliance on your word. Whenever I ſuggeſted a doubt of the other Proprietors, you aſſured me you could and would command for me a majority upon all occaſions; and, (notwithſtanding you have broken all your engagements with me, though I have incontrovertably convicted you, from your own words, of a conduct ſcandalous from its fallacy, diſgraceful

from

ſrom its diſhonor, and contemptible from its meanneſs) you at this moment proſeſs yourſelf my friend.

Having been ſo long in the habit of relying on ſuch ſerious and ſolemn promiſes, ſo often reiterated, and given ſo unſolicited, I have moments when, I flatter myſelf, you yet mean to keep them; when, your heart having ſufficiently upbraided you with your deſpicable treatment of me, and ſhewn you how difficult it will be, after this tranſaction, to perſuade other men to truſt you, you mean nobly to make one generous ſtruggle, one honourable effort to redeem the ninety-nine ſins of hypocriſy that are paſt, by one repentant ray of honeſty to come.

In anxious expectation of the appearance of your *latent virtue*,

I am,

With every deference and reſpect due to *ſuch a benefactor*,

SIR,

Your moſt humble ſervant,

C. DIBDIN.

Advertisement.

HAVING shewn this production to many of my literary friends, I am favoured in return with some *Jeu des Esprits* from almost every one of them, together with the liberty of inserting it in addition to my pamphlet.

First giving them my public thanks for the kindness of sanctioning my cause with their better labours, I shall prefix these elegant trifles to the work in the same order, as it was formerly the custom to publish commendatory verses, which, in more instances than this, have been found to make up the best part of the readers entertainment, and, like the superb frame of an indifferent picture, attract more notice than the painting itself.

The

THE HUMBLE

Petition *of* Common Senſe,

TO THE

Proprietors *of the* Royal Circus,

Sheweth,

THAT your petitioner was born of honeſt and reſpectable parents, Reaſon being your petitioner's father, and Prudence her mother.

That your petitioner humbly conceives, in her dealings with all mankind, ſhe hath rather done good than harm.

That the influence of your petitioner, on the conduct of thoſe connected in public concerns, hath in particular been always found productive of profit and reputation.

That your petitioner had once the pleasure of belonging to the Royal Circus.

That your petitioner, by the malice of her enemies, hath undeservedly incurred your displeasure, and hath, without a fair opportunity of vindicating herself, been disgracefully dismissed from your service.

That your petitioner's conduct hath been unexceptionable.

That your petitioner hath kept no bad company, Good Order and Propriety being her only companions

That your petitioner hath been attentive to your interest, strenuous in your defence, and anxious to promote your welfare.

That your petitioner's advice hath always been productive of advantage to the concern; that it hath always been found good policy to follow it, Common Sense being nearly allied to Honesty.

That

That your petitioner plainly sees Folly hath usurped her place.

That your petitioner wishes to warn you, that Folly hath about her a number of incendiaries, such as Conceit, Self-opinion, Bad Taste, and Ignorance, who, if not guarded against, will prove the destruction of the Royal Circus.

That these incendiaries, who are headed by Obstinacy, will represent matters through false and artful mediums.

That they will make derry down sound like an Italian air, rags appear like embroidery, counters shine like guineas, and empty benches seem to have persons sitting upon them.

That these incendiaries will deceive you in a variety of other instances, till, having led you on like a Will o' th' Wisp, or an *Ignis Fratuus*, you will at last find yourselves fast in the mire.

That your petitioner, more for your own interest than her's, wishes to be restored.

That

That your petitioner is well aware, without her aſſiſtance the Royal Circus muſt ſhut up.

That your petitioner conceives, of your own accord, you ought to diſmiſs Folly and Obſtinacy from your councils for ever.

That your petitioner hath not been uſed to entreat, but, at the inſtance of Pity, who hath a regard for you, ſhe hath been prevailed upon tc preſent this petition.

That, leaving all theſe matters for your conſideration, your petitioner humbly hopes you will open your eyes, and receive her into the Royal Circus;

And your petitioner, as in duty bound, ſhall pray.

THE

E P I G R A M.

FABIUS, a ſurgeon once, now wealthy grown,
His former pot-companions ſcarce will own.
One, Tim by name, more nettled than the reſt,
Hands up his friend in a ſatiric jeſt;
Tells how, with conſcience far more wiſe than nice,
Fabius his fortune made by loaded dice.
"You've cut him up," cries one, "all's right," ſays Tim,
"He formerly cut me—now I cut him."

E P I G R A M

IF he the cruel torture could ſurvive,
What muſt the poor wretch ſuffer flayed alive,
And after whipt?—But what feels D—s then,
Firſt conſcience flay'd, then laſh'd by D——n's pen?

A MORAL COMPARISON.

VIPER was told, 'twas a good thing to cheat,
That cards and loaded dice made ſmall men great
Viper apprentice put him to the trade
Firſt learn'd to cut a heart, next ſlip a ſpade;
'Till bolder in nefarious practice grown
Of all true gamblers, none about the town
Could cog like him, or for a pidgeon poach
How has it ended?—Viper keeps his coach

He pilfer'd in a petty pidling way :
Of wipes all ſorts rum codgers would unload,
'Till perfect in his trade, Dick takes the road,
Cries ſtand, leaps turnpike gates, defies the Bench,
Queers the rum cull, and keeps a handſome wench.
O partial fate! to ſee near Viper's palace,
Honeſter Scraggins ſcragged upon a gallows!

A DISPUTE *between* JEW BAIL *and* JEW FRIENDSHIP

BLACK WILL for Jew bail to the city was gone,
To poſtpone a Jew cauſe for his crony, Sir John;
High were Moſes' demands, — 'Te tings cout pe tone,
'Put twout coſht'—"Zounds," cries Will, almoſt angry grown,
"You've a bail in our debt."—'No, tiſh not in te pont'
"Then pay back the money"—'I nefer refont'
"Why, you promis'd'—'A promiſh betwixt me and you!'
"Ye gods, can I bear it—compar'd to a Jew!"
'Ten times worſh, I put prouniſht to fint you coot pail's,
'You to make your friendſh fortune, den ſhent him to chains.'

The

The Equeſtrian Creed.

WHOEVER would belong to the Royal Circus, before all things it is neceſſary that he hold the proprietors infallible.

Which infallibility, unleſs he keep abſolute and unequivocal, without doubt he ſhall periſh in the King's Bench.*

And the proprietors infallibility is this, that we flatter one perſon in five, and five in one, neither confounding the perſon, or dividing their committées; for there is one perſon of the city, another of St. Thomas's Hoſpital, another of Newmarket, another of the Court, and another of Weſtminſter Hall.

But the merchant, the ſurgeon, the ſportſman, the courtier, and the attorney is all one: the ſtupidity is equal, the abſurdity eternal.

* Since this was written Mr Dibdin has been additionally perſecuted, by being removed with a Habeas to the Fleet.

Such

Such as the merchant is, so is the surgeon; and such is the sportsman, the courtier, and the attorney.

The merchant stupid, the surgeon stupid, the sportsman stupid, the courtier stupid, and the attorney stupid.

The merchant absurd, the surgeon absurd, the sportsman absurd, the courtier absurd, the attorney absurd.

The merchant incomprehensible, the surgeon incomprehensible, the courtier incomprehensible, the attorney incomprehensible.

And yet not only one is stupid, they are all stupid.

Neither is only one absurd, or one incomprehensible, they are all absurd, and all incomprehensible.

So likewise the merchant is a committee, the surgeon a committee, the sportsman a committee, the courtier a committee, the attorney a committee,

And

And yet there are not five committees, but one committee.

So the merchant is manager, the surgeon manager, the sportsman manager, the courtier manager, the attorney manager;

And yet there are not five managers, but one manager.

So the merchant is a music-master, the surgeon a music-master, the sportsman a music-master, the courtier a music-master, the attorney a music-master;

Yet are there not five music-masters, but one music-master.

For, as we are compelled by Common Sense to acknowledge every person to be what he is,

So are we forbidden by the Equestrian Creed to acknowledge any proprietor but for what he is not.

The

The merchant is no committee, for he is never in committee-room.

The ſurgeon is no committee, for he ſigns reſolutions without agreeing to them.

The ſportſman is no committee, for were he to ſign, he could not underſtand the reſolution.

The courtier is no committee, he not being a proprietor, but the repreſentative of a proprietor.

The attorney is not a committee, he being the treaſurer.

Likewiſe the merchant is not a manager, but an accomptant.

Neither is the ſurgeon a manager, but a horſe-racer.

Neither is the ſportſman a manager, but a cock-fighter.

Nor

Nor is the courtier a manager, but an elegant lounger.

Neither is the attorney a manager, but a writer of tautology.

Likewise the merchant is no music-master, he having no ear.

Neither is the surgeon a music-master, he having no taste.

Neither is the sportsman a music-master, he preferring a Jew's harp to a Cremona.

Neither is the courtier a music-master, but a *Dilletante*.

Neither is the attorney a music-master, he having no harmony in his soul.

Yet are they all committees, all managers, and all music-masters.

And in this concern none is before or after the other, none is greater or less than the other.

But

But the whole five proprietors are equally ſtupid, equally abſurd, equally incomprehenſible, and equally infallible.

Yet has each a better fortune than the other; each is a better merchant, ſurgeon, ſportſman, courtier, and attorney, than the other, and each is a better committee-man, manager, and muſic-maſter, than the other.

Alſo each is a better fiddler, a better painter, a better carpenter, a better horſe-rider, and a better figure-dancer, than the other.

Each is ignorant, yet each poſſeſſes all kind of knowledge.

Each is black and each is white, each is vulgar and each is genteel.

So that in all things as aforeſaid, the proprietors muſt be flattered, their folly muſt be flattered, their vanity muſt be flattered, and above all, their flatterers muſt flatter themſelves with a belief of their infallibility.

And he who would belong to the Circus, muſt thus think of the proprietors.

THE

ROYAL CIRCUS

EPITOMIZED.

WHEN a man has received boundleſs obligations from the public, when the labours of his life have been at their devotion, and they have favoured him in return with the ample recompence of profit and reputation, he ought to view his own intentions with the niceſt circumſpection, and to be convinced he can ſafely determine to keep truth in conſtant view, before he officiouſly calls on the world to judge of his private concerns.

Upon this ground I am willing to ſtand. I have preſented the public at different periods with nearly ſixty pieces * of which I am author and compoſer, beſide the muſic of eight or ten others, and out of all thoſe only three have been unſucceſsful. Thus, the flattering applauſe with which my efforts have been indulgently favoured, would ſtamp me unworthy of future notice, if in the preſent relation I dared to obtrude any thing falſe or futile. The candid public has ever had a pride in taking up the cauſe of an injured individual, no man can more truly anſwer that deſcription than myſelf. I am inhumanly and cauſeleſsly perſecuted, hunted from my liberty, and ſuſpended from holding a legal right, for no other fault than having relied upon the ſuppoſed honour of a ſet of men who were ſtrangers to that word. I am now irritated, by calumny and oppreſſion, to that appeal which it is peculiarly my province to make. The laws will realize the truth of my claim, but it is the public I proudly aſk to decide upon the integrity of my intentions.

* See laſt page.

The

The neceſſity of adverting to every circumſtance which may poſitively or preſumtively tend to ſubſtantiate the facts in the following narrative, makes it impoſſible to avoid giving a brief hiſtory of the Circus and its origin. This, however, as it has long been a ſubject of public converſation, may not prove unentertaining, no place having been more internally convulſed, or ſtruggled through more diſtraction, nor is it wonderful. It was begot at Newmarket, born in St. George's Fields, and nurſed in Bridewell, till falling into bad company at the Opera Houſe, it deſpiſed the advice of its tutor, aped all the faſhionable abſurdities, and at laſt emancipated from the puling childiſhneſs of reaſon and plunged into the full maturity of folly at the Cockpit Royal.

In the month of February, 1782, having previouſly imparted my intention to Mr. Hughes, I applied to Mr. Davis, of Bury-ſtreet, St. James's, to build a place which I intended to call the Royal Circus; offering him a fourth of the profits which ſhould accrue from the amuſements there intended to be exhibited. He took but four and twenty hours to determine, for in that time he had communicated the bufinefs to Mr. James Grant, late of Coleman-ftreet, Mr. George Grant, of America-fquare, and Mr. Harborne, then of Amen-corner, but fince of John-ftreet, Adelphi; who having the higheft opinion of the plan I had given them, agreed, in conjunction with Mr. Davis, to fubfcribe fufficient money to erect the building, and that I fhould be its fuperintendant and uncontroulable manager; that they would receive the fourth I had offered as a compenfation for laying out their money; that Mr. Hughes fhould have one-third for his performance and breaking horfes; and that I fhould have the remaining five-twelfths, the one-twelfth more than Mr. Hughes's proportion being adjudged me for my trouble as manager.

Mr. Hughes was to provide horfes at his own expence, and I was to prepare the fcenes at mine; all other out-goings of every denomination the proprietors were to pay.

The

The leafes of the Magdalen Coffee-houfe and the two houfes adjoining were immediately purchafed with a view to erect the building in their ftead; but finding the place inconvenient, an application was made to Temple Weft, Efq. (fince dead) of Charlotte-ftreet, Rathbone-place, who owned the reverfion of an oppofite piece of ground, and who, upon the condition of being received as a proprietor, confented to purchafe the life right of the then poffeffor, and let the ground to the four gentlemen above mentioned, himfelf alfo being a party.

The dimenfions of the building being determined on, and the heartieft concurrence given to every meafure, I fuggefted all parties to fet earneftly to work. Mr. Hughes fought out for performers, I did the fame. Upwards of twenty children were bound apprentices to Mr. Grimaldi, who I employed as ballet mafter, and who, by a memorandum of an agreement with me for the term of five years (in which we mutually covenanted to enter into a fpecial article) promifed that the apprentices, then about to be bound to him, fhould not be employed at any other place

than

than the Royal Circus, and not there unlefs for my emolument, and by my order and direction.

In like manner I entered into an article under the penalty of £. 300 with the father of Mafter Ruffell, for three years, and two or three others at fhorter periods.

It was now thought a proper time to finally arrange our own articles, for which purpofe a meeting was had of the proprietors, Mr. Hughes and myfelf, where the fcheme being upon confiderably a larger fcale than the original intention, and the expence in confequence likely to be much higher, a frefh agreement was propofed to be entered into, by virtue of which the proprietors were to receive a third of the profit, Mr. Hughes the fame, (ftanding all his own expences) and I the remaining third, and to be allowed an annuity of £. 150 for managing, and to ftand at no expence whatever.

An article was ordered to be drawn up by Mr. Harborne, in which the parties were to agree, over and above the afore-metioned covenants,

covenants, that a committee, consisting of Mr. Harman, secretary and treasurer, on the part of the proprietors, Mr. Hughes and myself, should adjust and decide upon the current business, Mr. Harman having the casting vote if any dispute should arise between Mr. Hughes and me.

A licence, through the medium of Colonel West, was now applied for to the Duke of Manchester, which after an interval of some months was refused, it appearing very doubtful whether a sufficient power was vested in the Lord Chamberlain to permit a public entertainment beyond the precincts of the court, and his grace being young in office, was very tenacious of treading upon unprecedented ground.

It was now July, and no article drawn up, for which a variety of reasons were given. Mr. Harborne was represented as a man of such extensive business, that a failure in point of time on his part, ought to be considered as an admissible excuse; Mr. Davis repeatedly assured me, that on this account he was obliged to put up with the neglect of

private

private bufinefs of much greater magnitude; that nothing could exceed the fairnefs of their intentions, and I might be perfectly at eafe. Thefe very excufes alfo were held out to Col. Weft, whofe leafe and private agreement as proprietor were not executed. As I carried my good opinion of Mr. Davis to a pitch of enthufiafm, and for the fhort time I knew him, I had the higheft fentiments of Col. Weft's honour and integrity, this fatisfied me. Indeed every lover of truth muft revere his memory, for if a man of found and uncorruptible principles ever exifted, that man was Colonel Weft. He was befides wonderfully calculated to take a part in a public concern, he had judgment to difcover genius, and fpirit to encourage it; but it feems as if a fatality marked the wayward fteps of this unfortunate place; and becaufe there happened to be one man belonging to it who had tafte and liberality enough to refcue it from the barbarifm of arithmetic, the craft of chicane, or the defigning nicety of a gambling calculation, he muft be fnatched away, and the building be deprived of its ftrongeft prop and faireft ornament.

Mr.

Mr. Hughes, however, was leſs at eaſe than me, he apprehended, and very ſtrongly, ſome improper deſign on the part of the proprietors, nor did he ſcruple to aver that the buſineſs of the leaſe was held out as a falſe light to deceive us both, indeed, ſo freely did he broach theſe ſentiments, and in ſuch invidious terms, that being of an opinion totally oppoſite to his, I refuſed to ſpeak to him, except about mere buſineſs, for ſeveral months.

The mode of making deciſions in the committee was now totally altered, Mr. Harman not having for ſome time had a voice, but ſome one or other of the proprietors in his ſtead, for as the building advanced, it became a ſubject of amuſement to them, and they were as proud of owning themſelves parties concerned, as they were before ſhy of being known to have any thing to do with it, none of this I ever checked, but made it my ſtudy to pleaſe and ſatisfy them, little thinking I was teaching them the art of governing only to dethrone me.

In this, however, they have been a little premature; the theatical ſcepter, like a witch's ſpell, or a ſorcerer's taliſman, contains many figurative charms, which, if ill preſerved, or improperly uſed, only brings down confuſion on their heads, who have the temerity to tamper with them.

A licence having been refuſed by the Lord Chamberlain, the proprietors adviſed with Mr. Mingay how they could beſt apply to the Magiſtrates of the county for their permiſſion. They were informed by that gentleman, that the only time at which the bench could grant leave, was at the Michaelmas ſeſſions, he further cautioned them not to open the Circus, till ſuch conſent was obtained. This advice, however, I ventured to oppoſe the moment I heard it. Mr Mingay, as a counſel, was right. To fly in the face of the law, did not certainly appear the likelieſt means of obtaining its protection, but if he had had any eventual judgment concerning the probable fate of a new public place, his ſentiments muſt have been the reverſe, ſo much did I feel

feel the force of this, that I made no ſcruple to declare we ought immediately to open without a licence.

To ſupport this opinion, I gave the following reaſons: the intereſt that had been exerted to procure the licence from the Lord Chamberlain, together with the many preparations going forward, had not only exited univerſal curioſity, but raiſed ſome envy; the ſeeds of an oppoſition to the application at michaelmas were already ſown; theſe the world's ignorance of the ſcheme would be ſure to nouriſh, till they got to ſuch a head as to choke up all our hopes, proof of this came to us from ſome quarter or other every day; ſome reported that the place was built for tumbling and rope-dancing, and the introduction of drinking. Upon this ground I was ſure the magiſtracy would make a point of ſetting their faces againſt it, leſt it ſhould encourage idleneſs; others, who had heard Sir John Lade and Mr. Davis took a part in it, availed themſelves of the general opinion of thoſe gentlemen, by propagating that it was to be a receptacle for gambling.* The theatres naturally oppofed it, thinking a place prepared at fuch an expence might in the end rival them very formidably; all thefe difficulties I contended would be obviated by opening as foon as poffible. I argued, that let whoever would efpoufe our caufe, the town was at laft our beft protection and firmeft dependance. There if we found friends, we might laugh at private malignity, nay, that the very reports which were fo induftriously fpread, would recoil upon thofe who had the temerity to level them at us. What had we to do with fear? we were ourfelves confcious that nothing was intended but harmlefs amufements reprefented by children, which could not encourage diffipation; and which, fo far from militating againft the intereft of the threatres, would be found to be a nurfery for them, as the fchools of Oudinot and Nicholet are for thofe in Paris.

* At this time a paragraph appeared in one of the papers, giving a fuppofed opinion of the entertainments, where Sir John Lade and Mr. Davis were reflected on, in the way I allude to above, in pretty fevere terms.

I was

I was anſwered, if we had ſo many enemies, they would certainly take advantage of our opening without a licence, and inform againſt the place. I found no difficulty in pronouncing it would be the very beſt thing that could happen to us, we ſhould then ſee our danger, and know how to guard againſt it. That having confirmed ourſelves in the public good opinion, it would become a public cauſe. That the eligibility of the ſcheme, and the regularity with which it was intended to be conducted, would confound the tongue of ſcandal. The conſideration that ſo many children and their families were maintained by it, and other favourable appearances, would ſend the application to the ſeſſions upon ſuch fair ground, as could not fail to inſure it ſucceſs.

This advice operating contrary to my wiſhes, the work was ſlackened, and the place ordered to be got ready for October, inſtead of the following month.

For the firſt time, I began to diſcover a ſort of poſitiveneſs in moſt of the proprietors, to which I had hitherto been unaccuſtomed I did not like to thwart it, and yet I feared their perſiſting in error would terminate

an

in that very wilfulneſs which has been the deſtruction of almoſt every reaſonable meaſure hitherto propoſed. Contenting myſelf, however, with repreſenting the folly of their ſo ſtrenuouſly contending for a point, of which they had not experience enough to ſee the probable conſequences, and warning them that they would ſee my words verified, I gave up the matter, not without adviſing them to neglect no opportunity of gathering the ſenſe of the magiſtrates, previous to the ſeſſions.

The firſt ſtep they took towards this, was to give a public dinner, to which many of the gentlemen in the commiſſion of the peace were invited, none however attended, and this confirmed me ſtronger than ever, that my apprehenſions were but too well founded.

I now conceived it abſolutely neceſſary, that a memorial ſhould be drawn up, and preſented to the magiſtrates, by ſome one or other of the proprietors. The idea met their concurrence, and it was to be done immediately; but Mr. Davis and Mr. Harborne being continually in the country, neither of the Mr. Grant's attended for a long while,

and

and Col. West, most unfortunately for the concern, being taken ill, this necessary preliminary was neglected, and the licence when applied for lost by eighteen against fifteen affirmative voices, the greatest part of which majority declared themselves influenced against the application, by a letter which was read in court, written by order of the Secretary of State, to the Lord Lieutenant of the county of Surry, advising the bench to licence no new places of public entertainment, and this letter was actually procured, by a representation that the Circus was intended for E O tables, and every species of debauchery.

Thus, according to my prediction, the licence was lost by false and scandalous reports against the place, and clearly shews, corroborated by what really happened when the Circus was actually opened without any permission whatever, that had my advice been taken, we must have been successful.

Col. West continuing extreemly ill, the advantage of his advice was lost, and the other proprietors a good deal soured by their disappointment, were some time before they came to any resolution, at length my original

nal idea was adopted, and the place opened without a licence.

The world well recollects what encouragement the amuſements received, ſome of the firſt characters in the kingdom reſorted to the Circus, and it was conſidered as one of the moſt pleaſant and faſhionable places about town. The continual cry of the proprietors was, that I had done wonders, and that let what would be the fate of the concern, there was no degree of liberality that ſhould not be ſhewn me for ſuch uncommon and ſucceſsful exertions.

In all this time no article was prepared; and though I was unceaſingly teazed by Mr. Hughes, who went very great lengths indeed, and took moſt unwarrantable liberties with the proprietors names, to ſupport his aſſertions, though he even aſſured me, that they had conſulted together to diſmiſs me, though he called in Mr. Grimaldi to witneſs it, who declared, he had heard the proprietors ſay, they would never ſign an agreement with either me, or Mr. Hughes, this, and ten times more had not power to ſhake my opinion. I certainly was anxious that the matter ſhould

ſhould be finiſhed. I expoſtulated with Mr. Davis, and with Col. Weſt, on the ſubject; the firſt of whom *ſeemed*, and the other *was* as uneaſy as myſelf. Mr. Davis declared, that were the intentions of the other proprietors ſuch as Mr. Hughes and Mr. Grimaldi repreſented, yet his connections with them were of ſuch a kind, and his power over them ſo great, that he "could and would," (theſe were his words,) "command for me their majority upon all occaſions; but the fact was the very reverſe, the proprietors having the beſt intentions towards me." That the preparation of the article was only delayed by the negligence of Mr. Harborne, he laughed at my fears, and wondered how I could entertain them: muſt not he be void of honour, and merit the reproach of every honeſt man, if he could be capable of deluding me upon a ſubject ſo ſerious, ſo material to me?

I could not bear ſo many appeals to my feelings. I bluſhed that I had for a moment entertained an ill opinion of a man, than whom Lucifer or Iago would not have better acted the part of a friend. I conſidered Mr. Hughes and Mr. Grimaldi as two incendiaries, who, for selfish ends, were endeavouring to set me at variance with the proprietors, and I became more careless about the article than ever.

An information was laid against the Circus, and we were open only nine nights. My prophecy began now to be verified; all who had been our enemies became our warmest advocates; very distinguished persons consulted with us about opening again, and intelligence was given us from very powerful authority, that another application to the Lord Chamberlain would be successful.

The general expences, however, being all incurred, and the performers engaged, we thought it adviseable to open, if possible, upon some plan within the law, which we could extend, if we had the good fortune to succeed with the Lord Chamberlain, or continue (if the application failed) till the following October.

For this purpose, I devised a mode of amusement unlike any thing we had done before, which, sanctioned by counsels opinion, was brought out with success; but at the end

of

of the fifth night, a new information being laid, Mr. Hughes was taken up and sent to Bridewell.

In proportion as we were persecuted, so we gained friends. At the sessions, Mr. Hughes was honourably released, and the entertainment pronounced not to have been illegal. The application to the Lord Chamberlain went on rapidly, who being solicited in a very powerful manner, declared he would give a licence, if the Attorney-General would pronounce him competent to do it.

This business kept us on in anxious expectation till the latter end of February, when Mr. Hughes absolutely insisted on an article, without which, he declared, he would withdraw himself from the scheme.

I now began to find that this matter has been procrastinated only to beat us down in point of terms; for upon requiring so serious an explanation, it aukwardly came out that they had a good deal considered of it, and that in a different way than formerly. They now began to talk of the vast sums of money that had been laid out, of the loss the place had ſuſtained in throwing away ſo much time, that if no licence ſhould be obtained, or the concern involved in any future embarraſſment, they muſt bear all the burden. In ſhort, the new propoſal was, that Mr Hughes and I ſhould receive each a fourth of the profits, after paying all common expences, allowing them intereſt for their money, and a hundred a year ground-rent.

How did Mr Davis come off here? I am aſhamed to ſay with flying colours. He made it appear as plain to me, that I ſhould clear two thouſand a year for my life, as ever Breſlaw did one of his auditors, that he had conjured a ſhilling into his pocket, when the fact was, he had picked it of two, which were paid coming in at the door.

I did, however, muſter up ſo much clearſightedneſs, as to be a little uneaſy, not for fear the article ſhould not be ſigned, but leſt they ſhould pare away its value till it was not worth ſigning; and joining iſſue with Mr Hughes, never ceaſed importuning Mr. Davis, till, with the approbation of the proprietors, he ſigned a memorandum of an agreement,

in

in behalf of himſelf and the reſt, in the terms before mentioned, with the addition of tying up Mr. Hughes and myſelf from engaging at any other place of amuſement, and a promiſe of entering into a ſpecial agreement, as ſoon as it ſhould be found convenient to lay a proper deed before counſel. This memorandum was alſo ſigned by Mr. Hughes and myſelf, and witneſſed by Mr. Harman.

Whether the Attorney-General's opinion was never obtained, whether he was prevented from giving it, whether the intereſt uſed to get at the Lord Chamberlain was overturned by oppoſite influence, or whatever was the cauſe, I will not venture to pronounce my opinion; certain it is, we got no licence The matter has been ſo variouſly repreſented to me, that in relating what I have been told, I might very likely take a liberty with high and diſtinguiſhed characters, who, for ought I can with certainty advance, never heard of the Royal Circus but in common with the reſt of the world. Great names are very often uſed to ſerve little purpoſes, here they were uſed to no purpoſe at all.

This

This refusal determined us once more to open the Circus, merely to feel the pulse of the town, and to try whether all the pompous reports of our success among the great would not so far awe our enemies as to make them desist from any further persecution.

We did so, and it answered our end beyond expectation. The Circus was opened on the 15th of March, and it continued so without interruption till the middle of the following September; during all which time the sense of the memorandum was literally conformed to by the payment of a fourth of the profits to Mr. Hughes and myself every Saturday.

Soon after the Circus opened, Mr. Sewell, my Attorney and Solicitor, drew up a special deed, which was read by the proprietors, and (except the preamble and the mode of tying me to the Circus) approved of.

In Mr. Sewell's article, conformable to the memorandum, I was the acknowledged manager of the stage department for my life; my current conduct was to be decided upon by a weekly committee, which, so far from having a power to dismiss me from the Circus, was obliged to support and uphold me in it.

I should here mention, that just before this period, Mr. James Grant had sold his share to Sir John Lade, and Mr. Harborne had erected himself into the joint characters of treasurer, solicitor, and proprietor.

This circumstance did not create a little jealousy among the other proprietors, nor was it by any means a pleasant thing to either Mr. Hughes or myself, a proprietor being a very improper treasurer to a concern. This was represented at Sir John Lade's house, the Sunday before the place opened, Mr. Davis, Sir John Lade, Mr. Grant, Mr. Hughes, and myself present; and Mr Davis taking up the matter extremely warm, proposed the place for Mr. Savage, a gentleman we all knew, and of whose integrity we had the highest opinion. This met the wishes of every one present, and I expected to see him in his office the following Saturday; instead of whom, however, Mr. Harborne singly nomi-

minated

nated Mr. Grofmith, his brother-in-law; who has ever fince acted as a treafurer for him, and lately with the additional title of Secretary.

I only mention this circumftance, to fhew how completely the proprietors were ruled by the brilliant Mr Harborne; nor can it be wondered at I have already inftanced his *alacrity* in the difpatch of bufinefs, and when I come, in its place, to give a fpecimen of the elegance of his tafte, the winning fprightlinefs of his manner, and the captivating charms of his oratorical eloquence, the moft lively hopes may be entertained, that before the Circus fhall finifh its career, the world will fee him making out latitats upon three horfes, taking inftructions for a brief in a pantomime, or imitating the ferjeants when they make their bows at Weftminfter Hall in a *Minuet de la Cour*.

This fame Mr. Harborne, with infinite labour and pains (I think I fee him wiping his forehead) from the draft made out by Mr. Sewell, formed another, in which were introduced

duced many particulars totally foreign to the original intention. Neither Mr. Hughes nor myſelf was to have the liberty, without the conſent of a committee, to publiſh any book; that ſixty pounds a week were to be depoſited in his hands as a fund to pay all contingent expences. He nominated himſelf alſo perpetual treaſurer. The Committee was to have ſuch an abſolute power, that were they inclined to make vexatious and frivolous reſolutions, the concern muſt have been ſo harraſſed and perplexed, that no buſineſs of either Mr. Hughes's deparment or mine could poſſibly have gone on.

I not only ſaw all this, but that the prohibition of publications ſtruck particularly hard at me. It was repreſented to me, however, that no advantage ſhould be taken of me; that the article was ſo worded, leſt any nonſenſe of Mr. Hughes (I uſe the words of Mr. Davis and Mr. Harborne) ſhould be publiſhed to the diſgrace of the concern; that he was a man ſo troubleſome and unprincipled, and his conduct had been ſo reprehenſible, they were determined to have every poſſible curb on him, and particularly that the words and mufic of all my pieces were not implied in the claufe.

At this time another agreement was entered into by the Proprietors themfelves, to enforce the obfervance of their own private engagements. This deed is very material to my claim. It was executed by Colonel Weft, Mr. Davis, Mr. Harborne, Mr. George Grant, and Sir John Lade, and provided, among many other things, for the fecurity of the proceedings of a committee, by a claufe to the following effect: That fhould any of the Proprietors be inclined to fell a fhare, it fhould be offered at a ftipulated price to the reft, and that upon their refufal of the bargain, the buyer fhould be obliged to purchafe, fubject to all covenants and agreement whatfoever; and particularly that the prefent, as well as all future Proprietors, fhould be bound to keep, in the ftricteft fenfe, all engagements entered into with Mr. Hughes and myfelf. The memorandum recited above, which Mr. Davis entered into with the concurrence of the reft of the Proprietors, was figned previous to the execution of the agreement fome months. Will the fagacious Mr. Harborne

Harborne after this ſay he knew any thing of law when he ſigned my diſcharge from the Circus?

From the month of October, 1781, to this hour, (for it ſhould be underſtood that I had long ſuch a ſcheme in idea, though till February I could not find a perſon to take it in hand in any eligible way) I have received no emolument from any other place than the Circus. It will not therefore appear aſtoniſhing, that in ſuch a length of time I ſhould find it neceſſary, for my private purpoſes, to receive money on account from the Proprietors. I did ſo, previous to the 15th of March, to the amount of 261l. which ſum, together with every other expended or advanced for any purpoſe whatever, was agreed in the draft of the ſpecial article to go into a maſs, eſtimated at 12,000l. for which the concern was to pay ten per cent. intereſt.

I was in debt about 600l at the commencement of the ſcheme, ſome of which demands it would be very tedious and unpleaſant to explain; they were the dregs of former law-ſuits, penalties of engagements for a valuable and unfortunate relation, and ſome the con-

 ſequences

ſequences of follies committed twenty years ago; theſe debts, by the 15th of March, grew to 800l ſimply by the addition of law expences. The Circus now began to yield me very handſomely, and I had paid, by the month of July, near 400l.

About this time the remainder of my creditors began to perſecute me in a moſt rigorous and extraordinary manner; this appeared very ſingular, as they had received from me ſo much money, and more eſpecially as the loading me with law expences would only diminiſh my ability to ſatisfy them.

Upon ſearching into this buſineſs, I eaſily found they were ſet on; the Proprietors were of the ſame opinion, and made no ſcruple to pronounce Mr. Hughes the incendiary inſtrument; ſo much did Mr. Davis appear irritated at it, that he gave a promiſe to the officer, who was always upon theſe occaſions employed to arreſt me, that he would anſwer for every thing in future againſt me, that my perſon might be ſafe, and I might purſue my buſineſs in tranquility.

Why Mr. Davis refused to keep his word, the very next time I was arrested, he best knows.

The Circus about this time began to be one of the compleatest scenes of confusion that folly, ignorance, and interested art could plunge it into. The parents of the apprentices were eternally presenting me with petitions against Mr. Grimaldi; criminal accusations were preferred, addressed to religious lords; the magistrates interfered, and a compleat investigation into the morals and conduct of the place was ordered; some conscientious gentlemen in the commission, who had resolved right or wrong to vote against it the following October, were for its annihilation; and one in particular declared, he was so shocked at the idea of bringing up a number of children to the stage, that he should be afraid to meet them in the other world lest they should reproach him. The gentleman, I believe, did not consider that there would be no such danger, if that meeting happened to be in Heaven.

Three very reſpectable gentlemen were appointed inquiſitors upon this occaſion, whoſe great humanity, high honour, and unimpeachable integrity, are univerſally acknowledged. They found nothing that could induce them to take part againſt the place, and not only the accuſation fell to the ground, but the attempt to injure the ſcheme turned out materially to its advantage.

We were however the beſt judges of our internal commotions. Mr. Grimaldi's knowledge of the foibles of the Proprietors, his accommodating temper, and above all the ſecret manner in which he wormed himſelf into their favour to my prejudice, gloſſed over with them a number of moſt unpardonable faults, and it was in vain for me to order him upon any duty, when by a tale told to Mr. Harborne he could get himſelf excuſed.

As to the reſt, Mr. Hughes was evidently trying to get the place into his own hands, by harraſſing the Proprietors with accounts, in which they made no ſcruple to ſay they

were

were impoſed on, ordering dreſſes they diſap-
proved of, and uſing their names with moſt
licentious and unwarrantable freedom. All
this, together with his canvaſſing the county
in his name for the licence, and much other
indirect conduct, ſo alarmed the Proprietors,
that they were now the moſt anxious for the
articles; ſeveral meetings were had on it, and
at laſt Mr. Hughes, upon being paid all his
demands, agreed that the licence ſhould be
made out in his name and mine; and that
proper alterations being made in the mode
and manner of the article by Mr. Davis and
Mr. Pardon, the ſpirit of it, which had always been complied with, ſhould remain, and
then it ſhould be executed.

Thus matters continued in tolerable tranquility (except, as uſual, freſh law-ſuits being
conjured up againſt me; ſome legal, others
not ſo) till October.

The day came when we muſt apply for
the licence, and Mr. Hughes, after all that
had paſſed, inſiſted upon having it made out
in his name, or not at all. Nothing could
equal

equal the aſtoniſhment of the Proprietors at this demand; they fairly declared it ſhould have my name to it, as a check upon Mr. Hughes, or they would give up every concern with the place; that they had the higheſt opinion of my abilities, that my conduct had been fair, honeſt, and in every reſpect unexceptionable, whereas they believed Mr. Hughes to be guilty, in many inſtances, of proceedings directly the reverſe.

For my own part, I ſaw very plainly that the leaſt appearance of diſpute amongſt ourſelves would infallibly overturn our whole ſcheme, beſides, it was the cleareſt thing in the world that Mr. Hughes wrangled for no more than an additional feather to his equeſtrian helmet, which I was very well contented he ſhould wear. I argued, that while they were in contention for a mere name, the ſhadow of the buſineſs, they would loſe the licence, which was the ſubſtance, and that the place, and not the perſon, was the object of permiſſion. In this opinion Mr. Mingay joined me, the licence was aſked for in the name of Mr. Hughes, and granted.

During

During the meeting at Kingſton, our future operations were a ſubject of conſultation. As the place could now open by authority, as the entertainments would be entirely changed, by the introduction of burlettas and pantomimes, the orcheſtra thrown open, together with ſeveral other deſirable advantages, of which we might now avail ourſelves, I adviſed a recommencement of the amuſements. I nevertheleſs warned them how impoſſible it would be to keep open the whole winter; but in order to make it up to the performers, to take expence off the ſhoulders of the concern, and to provide novelty for the enſuing ſummer ſeaſon, I further adviſed an excurſion to Liverpool, Norwich, or ſome other capital place; there to wear out the old pieces, to be in the continual practice of new ones, and ſo come back at Eaſter with a fund of freſh dramatic materials, which would be ſo much variety ready prepared with little trouble, and no expence.

Nothing could be more eagerly catched at than this advice, it was ſo feaſible; ſuch a ſelf-evident advantage; ſo like generalſhip:

 Why,

Why, then, was not it adopted? The Proprietors of the Circus would not be consistent, if they were once in the right. They have a most tender affection for their own opinion; and as to obstinacy, no drove of pigs, in their journey from Berkshire to Smithfield, ever had such an aversion to a direct road.

Had my advice been taken, the Public would not now be nauseated at the Royal Circus (that place which once vied with the Opera-house; which, under the title of the Fairy World, enchanted its audience with all the magic of its name;) with the leavings of a barrel organ, the dregs of a porter club, or the refuse of Sadler's Wells.

Three or four days before we applied for the licence, the Circus and the world had the misfortune to lose Col. West, after having endured for near a twelvemonth all the torture and languor of a slow consuming wound, with a resignation and fortitude which, like all other of his actions, evinced his great mind. He dying, bequeathed wretchedness to his family, sorrow to all his connections, and regret to the memory of every man who

had

who had the happineſs and advantage of his acquaintance.

The Circus opened, and conſidering the expences of the receſs, the ſtock required to bring out the new things, and other incidental and unavoidable out-goings, did tolerably well. After a few weeks, however, it was decidedly clear that it would not do in the winter; this induced me to think in earneſt of the country ſcheme. I preſſed Mr. Hughes about it, who promiſed to write to Norwich, and propoſed it afreſh to the Proprietors, from whom I was aſtoniſhed to receive a cool anſwer.

I had now paid near 600l. to my creditors; and yet, ſo great a part of this ſum was for law expences, that I was ſtill in debt 450l. It is incredible, upon the failure of the ſucceſs of the Circus, how I was perſecuted, and all for trifles, which, by the management of bailiffs, evidently at the inſtance of Mr. Hughes, were magnified into things of conſequence. If I was to ſign a warrant of attorney, it was in his houſe; if I was arreſted, it was in his houſe. In ſhort, the moſt ſcan-

 dalous

dalous and illegal meaſures were taken purpoſely to expoſe me, and every illicit and vulgar manœuvre put in practice to injure my peace of mind, and render me incapable of doing my buſineſs.

So much did this appear the opinion of the Proprietors, that, to relieve my inconveniences at that time, they depoſited their draft of a hundred pounds in the hands of Mr. Sewell, and impowered him to inform my creditors, that they would be anſwerable for the payment of the reſt of my debts in a twelvemonth.

Mr. Davis promiſed to be preſent at the meeting of my creditors, inſtead of which, however, he wrote the following letter:

Copy of Mr. DAVIS'S FIRST LETTER.

SIR,

I AM very ſorry that I cannot meet you this evening in town, being obliged, on particular buſineſs, to go this afternoon to Maidenhead.

Maidenhead. I hope my abſence will be attended with no inconvenience; you know our ſentiments, and therefore you may propoſe to the creditors the mode which we ſettled. I believe I ſhall be in London to-morrow, and poſſibly I may have the pleaſure of meeting you at the Circus.

I am your humble ſervant,

WM. DAVIS.

Taplow, Wedneſday morning.

Stephen John Sewell, Eſq;
Golden-ſquare, London.

This letter being read, and Mr. Sewell explaining the ſentiments of Mr. Davis to be a determination to enter into the above agreement, the creditors were very well ſatisfied, and another meeting was propoſed, when Mr. Davis was to be preſent, and finiſh the buſineſs.

On the day of this meeting, however, Mr. Sewell received the following letter:

LETTER II.

SIR,

I AM ſorry to acquaint you, that Mr. Weſt, Mr. Grant, and Mr. Harborne, abſolutely

lutely decline to undertake to ſettle Mr. Dibdin's affairs, or to engage for the payment of any part of his debts. I am therefore, to my great mortification, in a minority of the Proprietors of the Circus, and have not the power of ſhewing my regard to Mr. Dibdin, by getting his buſineſs ſettled. I ſhall be glad of ſeeing you; and am your humble ſervant,

WM. DAVIS.

Stephen John Sewell, Eſq;

Notwithſtanding this ſhuffling, another gentleman of the law, as well as Mr. Sewell, adviſed the creditors to reſt contented, aſſuring them that the promiſe made by the Proprietors was binding in the ſtricteſt manner, even though not formally entered into, they having empowered Mr. Sewell to make it in their name. The creditors were ſatisfied with this, and went away, after being witneſs for one another that they would think no more of me, but ſeek their remedy againſt the Proprietors, at the end of the twelvemonth.

Mr. Davis has lately had the kindneſs to ſay, that as ſoon as Mr. Sewell, (who is contending for my right) ſhall have *done me a ſervice*,

vice, I shall write a pamphlet against him by way of thanks. I would ask Mr. Davis, if he himself ever did me a service, how comes it I am now in the King's Bench? and if Mr. Sewell is serving me, does not Mr. Davis confess his own consciousness of my re-establishment? The malignity of this caution to Mr. Sewell is too apparent. Mr. Davis knows how much it is his interest to prejudice my solicitor against me; fortunately, however, Mr. Sewell has too good an opinion of me to be wrought on by any such insinuations; and if he had not, his inveterate integrity in the discharge of his conduct to his clients, will ever induce him to take care of his honour and his character, than to suffer any craft or cunning to turn him aside from an honest discharge of his duty.

Mr. Sewell has suffered from Mr. Hughes almost as many indignities as I have, and wholly on my account. 'Tis a shame that Mr. Davis is not content with his treatment of me, without conniving at any dirty work of a man, whose name he has, in my hearing, a hundred times executed.

Three

Three of these creditors had actions against me, upon which I had been a long time held to bail; one of whom dropped all proceedings, but the other two went on at the commencement of the Term; being therefore incapable of paying the money: on the 21st of January, I was obliged to surrender myself to prison, to exonerate my bail.

It will appear very curious in this place, that when the Proprietors refused to fulfil their promise of paying my debts, they advised me to throw myself into the King's-Bench, offering to be security for the rules, and to give me apartments in the Circus; will it be credited then, after I had surrendered myself, they not only refused to be my security, but first voted me out of the Circus, and then used a secret influence to prevent my getting the rules at all. It is however very true; and though I hug myself at the good consequences that must result to me from their shallow, miserable policy, I cannot help feeling the malice and rancour of such a scandalous business, with that indignation in which I am sure every honest man must join me.

But,

But, as Macheath says, "It is a plain proof the world's all alike, and that even our gang can no more trust one another, than other people." Sorry I am that I have to reproach myself with belonging to that gang.

To clear my ground I must go back to about six weeks after the Circus opened, at which time a resolution was formed to shut it up, to open at Christmas, and then continue the entertainments if they should succeed. This I strongly opposed, recommending the country scheme; the Proprietors, however, confident of success, over-ruled me.

When the place came to be opened, matters turned out as I had represented them, even the first week did not bring its expences.

This caused such universal dissatisfaction, that every Saturday was expected to be the last of the season. Sir John Lade came to the Committee-room, and constantly blamed me for suffering the music to go ill, exhibiting such a curious and scientific system of criticism, as I sincerely believe, were it reduced to rule, would procure a sweepstakes to be run for in all the regularity of a *pas de quatre*— As well as edified by it, I should have been extremely amused, if it had not been embellished with some hints of properer managers, and the names of Grimaldi, Slingsby, Novoscielski, and others, occasionally dropped, "who were capable of bringing the whole world to the Circus."

Since however the place was so indifferently conducted, either it should not continue open, or the expences should be considerably lowered; he asked me first of all what part of the band I could spare? I said I could very ill spare any, but if it must be curtailed, I should begin with the trumpets. No, with a look of most ineffable contempt at my ignorance, he insisted on the trumpets being kept, even though *they should play by themselves*, for that they had a monstrous effect in recitative. As I knew I might as well have explained myself to one of his grey horses, and as I had more whims than his to please, I contented myself with tacitly striking

ing out the trumpets, and the names of a few uſeleſs performers, who had been only engaged in compliment to Mr. Hughes. Every preparation for novelty which happened to be in hand was next ordered to be ſtopped; painters, carpenters, and others, were to be diſcharged by wholeſale; and as we had low receipts, ſo we were to have low expences. It was in vain to repreſent that I could not produce new things without materials, I might uſe the old ones, that is to ſay, Tom Thumb might appear as an Alderman, Dollalolla as a witch, and the queen of the giants ſqueeze herſelf into the fly-jacket of a fairy. They however, at this moment, have recourſe to more miſerable expedients; for inſtead of thoſe dreſſes which induced the world to call the Circus the temple of taſte, the performers are ſtuck out in all the draggle-tail finery of a maſquerade at St. Giles's. Perhaps the Cyprian queen of that equeſtrian Adonis, Sir John, condeſcends to inſpire the wardrobe-keeper with the ſublimity of her taſte.

Nay, more impoſſibilities than theſe were exacted from me, I was to diſcharge the performers

formers (purpofely engaged for the new pieces) and then bring out the new pieces without them.

Expoftulating with Mr. Davis upon the abfurdity of all this, he told me not to regard any thing Sir John Lade faid, for that he was a man who would fet every body of people together by the ears he had any thing to do with.

On the other hand, my good ally, Mr. Hughes, was continually in confultation with his bofom friend and fecretary, Mr Stratford, (the bailiff who always arrefted me) how to make a finifh at once of me and my affairs: He made a violent entry into my houfe, and poffeffed himfelf forcibly in his rage, not only of all my property, but of the landlord's, without authority of any kind whatever, unlefs his having, againft my confent, undertook to pay money for me (evidently with a view of getting me into his power) can be fo called.

The Circus was now in a ftate of the moft complete diftraction; the very fervants faw I was not properly fupported by the proprietors,

 and

and therefore loſt all reſpect for me. In ſhort, all ſubordination was at an end; nor could the eloquence of the accompliſhed Mr. Harborne reſtore it, as will appear by the reception of the following oration, which well deſerves a title by itſelf.

ORATION *delivered by* RICHARD HARBORNE, *Eſq. to the leading-ſtringed Figure Dancers of the Royal Circus.*

Ladies and Gentlemen,

DO you know I am one of the proprietors? —My will here is to be a law; and if you do any thing wrong, I'll jerk you; I'll make you know your Lord God from Tom Bell.

A universal tittering immediately prevailed; the confuſion recommenced, and in five minutes the great Mr. Harborne was heard lamenting that his authority had not been able to awe one of the rebels, whom he detected, like Guy Faux, bearing a light to ſet off the fire-works before their time.

Within

Within a day or two of this memorable event, I came to the King's Bench; Mr. Davis gave his name as one of my securities for the rules, and suffered Mr. Sewell to make the usual enquiries; but being asked when he would sign the bond, answered not at all, because the rest of the proprietors had refused to join him.

I began to see the world now in a new light. I feared what Mr. Hughes and many others had told me of Mr. Davis (that he had not really been my friend, but appeared so by the consent of the other proprietors, the better to carry their measures) was but too true, the more especially as he had recently sold half his share to Mr. Grimaldi. To investigate this at once, I sent him the following letter and resolutions:

SIR,

MATTERS respecting the Circus having gone to a very alarming length, it becomes necessary that I should request the literal performance of those promises you have so often made

made me, and which as a friend, a man, and a gentleman, you are bound to abide by.

Through the whole progreſs of this buſineſs, it has been your uniform declaration to me, that I had a right to the fourth of the profits, and to conſider myſelf as the manager of the ſtage department at the Circus, fully and entirely ſubject only to the controul of a committee; and whenever I have expreſſed my fears of any unwillingneſs on the part of the proprietors to fulfil this agreement, you have diſſipated them by aſſuring me, that you could and would command a majority in my favour.

You have (empowered by a committee) ſigned a paper to the above effect; and, from the ſpirit of that paper, an article has been actually drawn, but not executed; and tho' I know, from the beſt authorities, that it is ſtrongly binding on the parties, yet from a natural wiſh to prevent litigation, I have frequently urged a formal perfecting of the neceſſary writings. Whenever I have done ſo, you

you have conſtantly aſſured me you would never ſell your ſhare, or any part of it, till you had ſeen every thing ſettled to my entire ſatisfaction.

You have very often, not only profeſſed yourſelf perfectly ſatisfied with my attention to the Circus, but have ever expreſſed an aſtoniſhment at my being able to furniſh it with ſo much variety, and when I was unjuſtly and cruelly harraſſed by my creditors, evidently through collateral and incendiary means, you gave it as your opinion, that no man was ever with ſo little reaſon ſo inhumanly perſecuted.

When we went to Kingſton, you had the higheſt ſenſe, according to your own declaration, of my talents and integrity; ſo much ſo, indeed, that you aſſured me you would rather loſe the licence than not have my name to it.

The world tells me, at this moment, that you are changed; that you look lightly upon all the promiſes you have formerly made,

and

and hold up your having parted with half your ſhare as a proof of it. My anſwer is, that 'tis impoſſible. That a breach of ſuch engagements would ſpeak you void of that honour on which I have ſo long relied, and which I give you an opportunity of vindicating, by entreating you to move the two reſolutions in the committee, which my brother (to whom I have given a power of attorney) will have the pleaſure of delivering to you.

I am, Sir,

Your moſt obedient ſervant,

King's Bench, C. DIBDIN.

Feb. 2, 1784.

W. Davis, Eſq, Bury-ſtreet, St. James's.

Reſolution 1ſt.

MR. DIBDIN having conceived it neceſſary, in conſequence of the change of ſome of the proprietors, to requeſt a reſolution of the committee, explaining his ſituation at the Circus: Reſolved, That he is conſidered, for the term of his natural life, as manager of the ſtage and all its entertainments, and allowed, for his trouble in conducting that depart-

H ment,

ment, a full fourth of all the profits ariſing from the receipts at the doors, after the expences are paid; ten per cent. intereſt allowed upon £. 12,000, and £. 100 a year for ground-rent.

Reſolution 2d.

Mr. Dibdin having requeſted, in conformity to the tenor of the ſubſiſting agreement, leave to write and compoſe an opera for one of the theatres, Reſolved, in conſideration of his preſent inconveniencies, that ſuch leave be given.

Theſe were intended to be delivered at the Cockpit while the proprietors were ſitting there in a committee; but apprehending, I ſuppoſe, ſomething of that ſort from me, the waiters had orders to ſay that there were not any proprietors there.

The letters, however, and reſolutions, were delivered to Mr. Davis, at his houſe, by Mr. Wilde, whom he told I had been the day before voted out of the Circus; that it was

a diſa disagreeable business; that he had no hand in it; owned to signing the memorandum, having given me his honour he would see me situated in the Circus to my wish, and, in short, every tittle I had charged him with in the letter. He said he supposed the matter would cost me a law suit, and heartily wished he could be of any service to me.

Thunderstruck with the intelligence of the vote, and very unsatisfied with the vague manner in which he seemed to get rid of my importunity, I wrote to him as follows.

SIR,

WHATEVER the proprietors of the Circus may have thought proper to resolve relative to me, I cannot admit such a measure in the smallest degree an extenuation of your having forfeited your promises. You have had the manliness to avow your having made those promises; have still the justice to see them fulfilled. They go to the very existence of my character, my public reputation and my private interest. I have rested on them with full confidence; for them I have slighted the advice of my friends, resisted every offer however eligible, and neglected (indeed my only neglect in this business, whatever false accusations may have been preferred against me) to insist upon the execution of a special article, which would have precluded all possibility of the very candid and gentleman-like vote which has so recently graced the immaculate committee-book of the Royal Circus. You will probably answer, that an action at law will reinstate me: I dare say it is your opinion, nay, upon perusing a paragragh of my former letter, you dropped a hint purporting so much. If this is the case, where was your friendship, where was your attention to my interest, when you had so fair a plea with your brother proprietors, and did not use it? Did they not authorise you to put your name to a memorandum stamping me manager of the Circus for my life? Here they have deserted you as well as me, and branded your name with the discredit of having been affixed to an agreement, which, spight of their former resolution, they here disavow. Was not

this

this the moment to command a majority?—Was not your natural anſwer,—Gentlemen, you have formerly authorized me to give this man the power he contends for, he has in conſequence a legal claim to it; and you ſhall not ſo far forfeit all pretenſions to juſtice, as to violate a ſolemn agreement, which, in your name, has my ſignature to it;—but, ſay they, you ſhall not have your way; ſo far from it, if even by law he reinſtates himſelf, we will ſhut up the place for ever, rather than ſuffer him to receive any emolument from it. —Why, ſays you, this is the moſt vindictive reſentment that ever was heard of, and levelled at me as much as the poor devil, the object of your perſecution: For, ſays you, if you ſhut up the Circus for ever, to ſpight him, I loſe the probable advantage in having laid out my money, and therefore ſhall alſo be compelled to go to law with you· Come, come, ſays you, do not be out of your ſenſes, you cannot vote him out; all the remedy, if he is guilty of neglect, is to bring an action at common law; but can you do this?—No; he has produced you ſince your licence three burlettas, one entire pantomime,

the

the music and words of another, three dances—altered, and fitted several other matters to the stage, and would be ready to bring out Tom Thumb, two French pieces, two dances, two new pantomimes, and a burletta for sailors, at the shortest notice, but that you have obliged him to discharge all his painters, will not suffer him to have new dresses, and, in short, incapacitated him from doing that which you falsely charge to his neglect.

It cannot fail to appear the most curious piece of ridiculous obstinacy that ever was agitated in a court of justice. Have I not letters from the proprietors respectively, recommending me fit persons to be engaged? Have I not existing articles under penalties? nay, is not even one of the proprietors, at this moment, engaged to me, and that by a written memorandum? In short, it is a measure big with that absurdity which has so long marked the conduct of this unfortunate place; and were not my feelings roused at its cruelty, and my indignation at its injustice, I could laugh at its imbecility, and pity its framers for the poor miserable flimsy pretext, behind which they were obliged

ged to ſkulk. What! be the fabricator of a ſcheme, give up two years and three months to it, be promiſed firſt very near half the profits, then a third and £. 150 a year, then content myſelf with a fourth, when the proprietors, if I cleared £. 1000 a year, would receive near thirty per cent. for their money, and a conſiderable advantage from poſſeſſing an accumulating ſtock, and ſuffer myſelf, after producing four or five and twenty pieces, to be voted out of a concern, which, from the evidence of all the world, was eſtabliſhed by thoſe very pieces? but my pleas againſt it are innumerable, and therefore I revert to my original poſition. You have ſuffered a majority to go againſt me, in that you have forfeited a promiſe which you were bound to both by friendſhip and honour. It is in vain to urge that you have but one voice, that you could not rule the opinions of others; I put all theſe objections at the time, and your reiterated anſwer was,—you could command a majority. I have ſtill hope to acknowledge you for that friend whoſe partiality to me gave me ſo much pleaſure; and that you will, for the ſake of your own honour, as

well

well as your good wishes for me, see that resolution rescinded, which, I will be bold to say, carries in the face of it not only injustice but ingratitude. This I expect from you; and nothing short of this can I be satisfied with.

I am, Sir,

Your most obedient servant,

King's Bench, Feb. 20, 1784.

C. DIBDIN.

W. Davis, Bury-street, St. James's.

The day after this, the following letter and resolutions were delivered to me from the Treasurer.

Mr Charles Dibdin,

BY the direction of the proprietors of the Royal Circus, I send you inclosed a copy of the resolutions entered into by them on the 3d instant.

At

At a Committee of the Proprietors of the Royal Circus, held at the Cockpit-Royal, February 3, 1784,

PRESENT,

William Davis, Eſq;
George Grant, Eſq;
Richard Harborne, Eſq;
Thomas Bullock, Eſq; for *Sir John Lade*,
Thomas Weſt, Eſq; for Mr. *Weſt*.

Among ſeveral other reſolutions, it was reſolved, That in conſequence of Mr Dibdin's having frequently, and for ſome weeks paſt in particular, neglected his duty as the deputy acting manager of the Royal Circus; and being now a priſoner in the King's Bench, whereby the buſineſs of the houſe in his department is wholly neglected, it is therefore abſolutely neceſſary, that the entertainments cloſe on Saturday next.

Reſolved, That, in conſequence of the above reſolution, notice be given to Mr. Dibdin, in the names of the proprietors, that they ſhall dispense with any further attendance of Mr. Dibdin at the Royal Circus, as the acting manager thereof, or any other engagement they have with Mr. Dibdin respecting the Royal Circus.

(Signed)

George Grant,
Richard Harborne,
For self and *Sir John Lade*, *Tho. Bullock*.
For Mr. *West*, *Thomas West*.

And in pursuance of their orders and those resolutions, I hereby give you notice, that you are dismissed from the management of the Royal Circus; and that your attendance there in future will be dispensed with.

I am, Sir,
Your humble servant,
C. GROSSMITH,
Secretary and Treasurer.

Royal Circus,
Feb. 10, 1784.

I was taught to expect this; therefore it brought me with it no surprise, not even the finding it such a master-piece of elegant composition.

position. The other proprietors, it was plain, had given me up. I could not, however, bring myself entirely to think the same of Mr. Davis: impatient for his answer to my last letter, I wrote to him once more.

SIR,

MR. WILDE has called on you several times for an answer to my letter, without the pleasure of finding you at home. You will please to send one by the bearer of this, or else leave it out for a messenger who shall call at your house on Monday morning; otherwise I must suppose, what will give me great pain, that you do not mean to keep your word of honour. At present I will not believe it possible, nor shall all I hear induce me to credit that you can look lightly upon such serious and solemn promises as those you made me, till you sanction the rumour by a refusal under your hand, or a continuation longer than Monday next of this contemptuous silence. I am, Sir,

Your most obedient servant,

C. DIBDIN.

King's Bench, Feb. 20, 1784.

At length I received from him the following letter:

SIR,

I never heard that Mr. Wilde had called at my houſe ſince he did me the favour to deliver your meſſage. I ſhould not have delayed for a moment the ſending an anſwer, if I could have written with a probability of mitigating in any degree the mortifications which you muſt receive in your diſagreeable ſituation, which I am truly ſorry for, but have not the power to redreſs.

The buſineſs of the Circus has been attended with a ſeries of perplexing ſituations previous to the laying the foundation of the building to this hour; hardly a week has paſſed without ſome new miſchief ariſing to perplex and involve the parties concerned in that unfortunate undertaking. At this time I find myſelf conſiderably above two thouſand pounds out of pocket, with a very poor proſpect of recovering any part of it. The other proprietors are in the ſame ſtate. The ſum

ſum of money expended is a matter of ſerious conſideration; and to have continued the undertaking a year or two longer in the looſe and extravagant manner in which it has hitherto been conducted, would have accumulated a debt that muſt have overwhelmed and brought ſome of the parties concerned to a priſon.

If I was diſpoſed to ſink every guinea I have in the Circus, it is not within my power to oblige the other proprietors to go the ſame length with me. Your conduct as manager of the undertaking was pronounced the cauſe of the failure of the Circus; and being ſcrutinized by four out of five of the proprietors, has been thought ſufficiently reprehenſible for them to vote your expulſion. You know that a majority determines all matters of buſineſs relative to the Circus, therefore my ſingle vote, had I given it, would have anſwered no purpoſe.

I need not ſay that I entertain the higheſt opinion of your abilities; the alacrity I have ſhewn in advancing my money to carry on the ſcheme in St. George's Fields, and the trouble

ble I have taken to forward the buſineſs, ſpeak fully to that point. As a friend, and a very old acquaintance, I ſhould have had infinite ſatisfaction if the project had anſwered your expectation; and I am very ſorry that your conduct has loſt you the confidence of the proprietors, who, you muſt confeſs, readily embarked, and in a moſt liberal manner ſubſcribed, to an undertaking, which, properly managed, would not have failed to have made a moderate return to them, and placed you in an affluent ſituation. The failure of it has ſo far diſguſted me, that I am determined to avoid, as much as poſſible, every interference in the buſineſs, and to ſubject myſelf hereafter to as little trouble and loſs as the caſe will admit. I am, Sir, lamenting your misfortunes,

Your friend and humble ſervant,

Bury-ſtreet, WM. DAVIS.
Feb. 23, 1784.

Charles Dibdin, Eſq,

So much evaſion opened my eyes; I felt myſelf duped, and what was worſe, I felt I deſerved it: comforting myſelf, however, with the reflection, that *being* was ſomething more honourable

honourable than *having* deceived, I wrote him the following letter.

SIR,

I HAVE read your letter of the 23d with much attention, but fpight of my eager inclination to find in it any thing like friendfhip, kindnefs, or liberality, I difcover only polite invective, plaufible evafion, infulting civility, a haughty, cruel confcioufnefs of the independence of your fituation, and an overftrained commiferation for the lownefs of mine. By this letter I am convinced of what I have been fo often told, and would never believe, that your profeffions of friendfhip were a bubble blown up to amufe me, and which would leave me nothing fubftantial but the mortifying knowledge of my own egregious folly; you fhall excufe me, therefore, feeling it rather hard to fubfcribe myfelf your dupe, if in pretty bold language I take the liberty to anfwer it. I well know that the bufinefs of the Circus has been attended with a feries of perplexing fituations—that you have advanced above 2000l.—that my con-

duct

duct as manager of the concern has been pronounced the caufe of the failure of the Circus—that two out of five of the Proprietors have voted my expulfion—for I do not acknowledge the competency of Mr. Bullock or Mr. Weft—that a majority are to determine all matters of bufinefs—that you have an opinion of my abilities—that you would have been glad had the project anfwered my expectation—that had it been properly managed it would have placed me in an affluent fituation—and that you are forry for and lament my misfortunes: But I know, and fo do you, that I am not the caufe of the Circus's perplexities—that though you have advanced, you are not out of pocket 2000l.—that mine has been the only confiftent or proper conduct in the whole concern—that the expulfion of the acknowledged manager for life is not a matter of bufinefs, but a thing impoffible to be done; therefore had your affent given it fanction, the vote would have amounted to nothing—that however you may rate my portion of abilities, you think I have ftill a larger one of credulity—that an affluent fituation to me would have been rather more than a moderate return to the

the Proprietors; the first ten per cent. being theirs, a hundred a year ground rent, a full half of the profits (which in six months cleared them 1800l.) the buildings, the improvements, and the accumulating stock; and lastly, you know that your sorrow and lamentations over my misfortunes are no more than a conscious reflection that you are the cause of them. It will scarcely be believed, that to usurp my dramatic throne, and send me to this indignant exile, so flimsy, so poor, so bungling a pretext, as that of neglect, should be pitched upon. My judges, like those of Socrates, are determined to condemn me right or wrong; this villainous philosopher, say the latter, knows us too well, he speaks profanely of our idols; he is a good man, to be sure, the whole world admires him; but since it will only expose our own ignorance, or perhaps something worse, to investigate the truth, let him die unheard. Thus say the Proprietors, there is no harm in this man, we have the highest opinion of his abilities, he has devoted more than two years to the Circus, and we declared only last October, that, if the licence was not made out in his name,

ject should be ruined; but, say the Pro-
prietors, we know beſt our own reaſons why we wiſh to part with him; be it then reſolved, that he is guilty of neglect—of neglect, echoes the Treaſurer—Oh! he's a ſad negligent dog, cries his very aſſiduous and worthy colleague;—neglect loſt you the confidence of the Proprietors, reiterates in pathetic ſtrains the compaſſionate and friendly letter of Mr. Davis. Thus Socrates ſwallowed the hemlock, and I am expelled the Circus. Mine, however, is no more than a theatrical death; and you may be aſſured, when the curtain has dropped upon your farce, I ſhall riſe again, and perform my part with more vigour than ever. To one ſpecies of neglect I am ready to plead guilty, that neglect of having taken good care of myſelf; of having inſiſted on mens bonds, whoſe words were not to be truſted, and of receiving from you as a man of buſineſs, that which, under the maſk of friendſhip, you promiſed, without intention of performing.

But that I have failed to promote and forward the buſineſs of the Circus, or attended it with an aſſiduity beyond all example, I defy

any

any of you to prove. If, however, it ſhould appear, contrary to the kind expectation of thoſe characters ſo remarkable for liberality, that I am not totally ruined, but able to procure the means of carrying on an expenſive ſuit, this point a Court of Juſtice will illucidate, there the terrific menaces which uſed to ſcare little children behind the ſcenes,* make fidlers tremble in their orcheſtra, hair-dreſſers drop their curling-irons with aſtoniſhment, and fright the Circus from its propriety, like ugly vizors at the hour of unmaſking, will vaniſh with all their diſtortion, and diſcover harmleſs, inſipid countenances, looking for gratification, and finding diſappointment.

I ſhall, however, anticipate no argument intended for the mouth of my counſel, but content myſelf with ſhewing you, in a much ſtronger light than I have hitherto repreſented the matter, that you either have it in your power to do me juſtice, or you muſt be oblig- ed to confeſs yourſelf guilty of a premeditated

* Alluding to Mr Harborne's Oration, which ſee in its place

bafenefs, neither confiftent with the character of a gentleman, or a man of honour.

When the draft of the fpecial agreement was delayed, and I apprehended fome unpleafant confequences, to quit me of my fears you made me this declaration.—Be perfectly eafy, I do not fay that the very words of that agreement which Mr. Sewell has drawn up fhall ftand in that to be executed. but it is fettled among us, that the fpirit of that article fhall be faithfully adhered to, and all the emoluments and advantages there fet down fhall be infured to you, and this declaration you prefaced with the following remarkable words.—" If you can prove that I ever told a ferious lie, I give you leave to call me the greateft villain that ever exifted" With the *fame* preface, alfo, you made me a declaration, when it was reported you were about to part with your fhare, that you embarked in the bufinefs to ferve me; that you would fee me eftablifhed in it for life, and that fooner than fell your fhare, or any part of it, the Circus fhould bring you to the King's Bench. No fuch fpecial agreement has been figned; you have fold a part of your fhare; the application is obvious;

obvious; you are—but gratitude forbid that I should wound the bosom of my friend. What possible reason, then, can be given for this extraordinary conduct? I'll tell you; to give eligibility to your place; to learn the trade of conducting it, to possess yourselves of a stock of dramatic materials, I was gulled by promised mountains, which only brought forth real mice; till having gained your point, you violently, against reason, honour, or law, dispossess me of my situation, with a view of adding my fourth of the profits to your half; backed with a self-assurance that I am too poor to right myself. But could you have carried your point, where were the talents to come from to have supplied the Public with variety? Are they to be found among all that glorious confusion of parchment, cobwebs, and sealing-wax, which envelope the muffatees of the elegant and erudite Mr. Harborne? In Mr Grant's exemplication of tare and tret, Mr. West's drawing-room, your improvement upon Hoyle, or Sir John Lade's study of cock-fighting? Or have you found it in that heap of jarring matter the dancers, fidlers, furies, and castratos of the Opera-house? and so think, as a theatre is an epitome

of

of the world, that it can not arrive to order, 'till it has ſprung out of chaos. However, like the general conſequence in all ſuch caſes, you have been too cunning for yourſelves; the memorandum, Mr. Davis, to which you ſet your hand, will ſpeak for me in ſuch terms, as ſhall oblige you to do me legal juſtice. That due to my honour, I ſhall take care of myſelf. Be aſſured, therefore, I have no fears of righting myſelf, in ſpight of the curious and probable ſtories propagated by the Proprietors, their honeſt and gentleman-like vote, or your facetious ſentimental letter; which, like the fiddle of Nero, at the deſtruction of Rome, is the inſtrument of your mirth, at the ſight of my misfortunes.

I am, Sir,

Your humble ſervant,

King's Bench, C. DIBDIN.
Feb. 25, 1784.

The next news I heard was, that Mr. Grimaldi had the appointment of Manager in my ſtead, and that Mr. Davis took by the hand that very Mr. Grimaldi, who he himſelf

told

told me had endeavoured to poison the minds of the Proprietors against me; who he knew to have been guilty of very improper conduct; who he pretended he had the worst opinion of, and who he detested, on account of his underhand treatment of me. As to Mr. Grimaldi himself, he had made a parade of declaring, that he conceived himself under the highest obligations to me; that I had given him his bread at the Circus, and he would rather die, than do any thing that could militate against my interest, he, too, had a particular fancy to being called rascal, whenever he deceived me, but he need not be uneasy for me, he shall peculate in peace, and safely carry his crazy bones to that grave which yawns for them, where the highest compliment mankind can pay his ashes, will be to throw on his memory the veil of oblivion.

I shall detain the reader no longer than while I examine whether it appears that I neglected my duty at the Circus; whether, had that been the case, the Proprietors were competent to dismiss me, and whether, by having voted me out, they have advantaged themselves?

To

To the charge of neglect I answer, that I have given an induſtry ſo indefatigable, an attention ſo unremitted, that till laſt Chriſtmas the Proprietors expreſſed an aſtoniſhment at my perſeverance. I can ſafely ſay, I devoted ſix hours in every day, upon an average, for near two years and a half, to ſupplying the Circus with materials; for I have not neglected to do ſo even to this moment. I actually brought out there twenty-eight performances, twenty-one of which were entirely new. I wrote all advertiſements, drew up ſeveral memorials and petitions, and gave directions in every department, except relative to the horſes, for two years; nor out of the whole number of nights the Circus was opened, did I abſent myſelf more than about fifteen times, the major part of which omiſſions was owing to the broken promiſes of Mr. Davis, in the name of the Proprietors, to my creditors.

A further way to ſee if I have been negligent, is to examine my conduct and Mr. Hughes's together. Have not the Proprietors complained, from the firſt moment to the laſt,

laſt, that nothing could induce Mr. Hughes to produce any ſingle novelty? Did I not project ſeveral things for him? Are there not materials for this uſe, prepared by my directions, as far back as July, 1782? And do not the Proprietors well know that one of my greateſt difficulties was continually to torture words into a variety of meanings, differently to announce old manœuvres in new advertiſements. Is this the caſe in relation to me?—ſo far from it, that, beſides what I have already mentioned, ſo much had I the intereſt of the place at heart, that when they were determined to open at Chriſtmas, and I felt it could never do, I offered (without any emolument whatever, notwithſtanding I had long made a determination to the contrary, and thereby certainly given up many an advantageous ſituation) to write burlettas in a new ſtile, and *perform in them myſelf.* Nay, being well convinced of the impoſſibility of their providing proper novelty for the commencement of their ſeaſon, I have repeatedly given them notice of many new performances that are actually now by me, and any three of which might have been performed on laſt

L Eaſter

Eaſter Monday; but they did not even deign to anſwer theſe notices.

It will eaſily be ſeen then that I did ſomething more than Mr. Hughes; however I will do him the juſtice to ſay, that if I did my utmoſt, ſo did he his.

Can this conduct then be called neglect, or is this a proper return to it? Is the exiſtence of a man in good profeſſional eſtimation thus to be ſported with? Is he to throw away two years of his time in fabricating a ſcheme, ſupplying it with materials, watching the growth of its improvements, ſuperintending and even teaching the performers, and giving it every advantage, perfectneſs, and conſequence? Is he to leſſen the reputation of his muſic by ſuffering children to perform it, inſtead of capital ſingers at the theatres? Is he to ſhut himſelf out from every other concern, to decline all applications that have been and are now made to him? Is he to take back accepted pieces from the theatres, which were ſure to yield him conſiderable profit? and is it reaſonable that all this care and pains, loſs, and retirement from his former conſequence, ſhould

ſhould be rewarded by an expulſion from the very concern that but for him never would have had exiſtence.

The Circus did not apply to me! I found no ſuch place ready built to my hands! I projected it, fabricated it; it was the child of my own fancy; it was the harbour wherein I meant to moor my bark, as a haven againſt all the tempeſts of fortune. Who could have believed that the inſidious pilot who ſteered me to it ſhould be the firſt, after unlading my cargo, to ſet me adrift to the buffeting waves of adverſity, and the mercileſs winds of oppreſſion!

As to the competency of the Proprietors to vote me out of the Circus, unleſs contracts between man and man may be broken at will, the good faith and ingenuous reliance of one man upon the common honeſty of another violated at pleaſure, and mens names ſuffered to be affixed to paper merely as a mockery of juſtice, that competency I think will not be eaſily proved

The Proprietors will not deny that it was a very common thing for one of them to un-

 dertake

dertake for the reſt; they were collectively liable as in matter of partnerſhip; Mr. Harborne has often accepted drafts for the concern, ſo has Mr. Davis, exactly in the manner he wrote his name to the memorandum, which inſtrument, like the agreement of a leaſe, is efficient till the leaſe itſelf is drawn up; and as a proof that the memorandum was compulſory, a ſpecial deed was actually prepared, and but that it exacted more than the agreement which compelled it, would have been ſigned.

As to the remaining queſtion, unleſs confuſion is better than order, ſtale performances more attractive than novelty, and empty houſes* more profitable than full ones, the Circus is not at this moment benefited by my abſence.

For the reſt, it is well the Proprietors can boaſt of the independency of their fortunes, ſince they have ſuch poverty of ſpirit. I cannot omit one caution, however: let it not be believed, becauſe thouſands are eaſily talked

* The difference of the profits this year and laſt, as I can prove by the receipts, is upon an average upwards of 180l. a week.

of,

of, ſuch immenſe ſums have been expended in the Circus as the world is taught to imagine; it coſt enough, and it is pity they had not paid dearer for the folly of neglecting wolesome advice.

Neither will it I hope be credited, that I have received upwards of 2000l. from the Circus, or that I am 3000l. in debt. Upon the faith and honour of a man, previous to laſt Auguſt, I had received no more than about 1100l. and ſince that time only 50l. or 60l. at moſt,* out of all which I paid near 700l. and maintained myſelf and my family ſince the month of October eighty-one; and I ſhould not at this moment owe more than 100l. had I not been embarraſſed as I before deſcribed, whereas I am indebted near five.

Thus have I brought this narrative to a concluſion. I pledge myſelf for the truth of it, and call upon the Public (the neglect of my duty to whom is of conſequence to me

* I cannot be exactly correct, for Mr. Hughes, by virtue of *the very legal* ſeizure he made in my houſe, is poſſeſſed of every private paper I had in the world.

indeed,

indeed, compared to the opinion of the Proprietors of the Circus) to brand me with ingratitude to them, and point me out as an object undeserving their future support, if I am detected of having advanced a single falsity.

Much subordinate matter, I confess, remains behind, which I thought unworthy of public inspection, but if the Proprietors feel bold, I throw down my guantlet, and dare them to meet me upon that, or any other ground. Indeed I believe, at this hour, if it was not for shame, they would send for me to meet them at the Circus They need not be unhappy; the law will do that for them, which they have not the resolution to do for themselves; and whenever it happens, they may be assured I shall be most unmercifully revenged of them, I will submit to no whim or caprice, but go on in the exercise of my own judgment. If I wish to expose the temple of chicane, lay open its rascally recesses, and rescue the innocent victims bound at its altars, I will not flinch from my design, even though Mr Harborne happens to be an attorney. I'll not scruple to tell the world, that horse-

racing

racing is not a moral duty; Pharoah, a syſtem of Philoſophy, or Cock-fighting, a ſtudy of humanity; even though Sir John Lade and Mr. Davis are gentlemen of the Turf. In ſhort, if inſtead of five I had five hundred Proprietors to deal with, all of different perſuaſions, profeſſions, and affections, I will boldly perſevere in furniſhing ſuch materials as I ſhall conceive moſt conduſive to amuſe the town, and profit the concern; nor will I conſider any neglect a crime, or bow to any correction, but that of the generous and candid Public.

F I N I S.

Lightning Source UK Ltd.
Milton Keynes UK
UKOW05f0646230816

281298UK00008B/116/P